Plants and How They Grow

by Kim Fields

PEARSON
Scott Foresman

DK

What are the main parts of a plant?

What All Living Things Need

Living things have needs. Plants and animals need food, air, water, and space to live and grow.

Animals need to find food to eat. Plants are different. They can make their own food. Plants use energy from the Sun to make food.

This Alaskan brown bear is looking for food.

Plants come in all sizes and shapes. They can grow almost anywhere. Each plant needs special things to grow. Most plants have four parts. Roots, a stem, flowers, and leaves are the four main parts.

These black-eyed Susans make their own food.

Why Plants Need Leaves

Plants need leaves to make food. The leaves make a type of sugar. A plant's leaves are a part of its leaf system. A **system** has parts that work together.

Carbon dioxide gas enters a plant through holes in the leaves. Water enters a plant through the roots. Leaves also take in sunlight. Water and carbon dioxide are changed into sugar and oxygen. The plant uses energy from sunlight to do this. The sugar is the plant's food. The oxygen goes out through holes in the leaves.

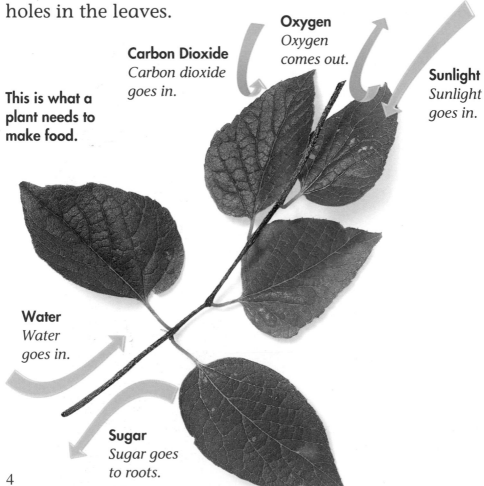

Oxygen
Oxygen comes out.

Carbon Dioxide
Carbon dioxide goes in.

Sunlight
Sunlight goes in.

This is what a plant needs to make food.

Water
Water goes in.

Sugar
Sugar goes to roots.

Other Ways Leaves Help Plants

Leaves also help control the amount of water in a plant. Leaves can let out extra water through tiny holes. A plant that lives in dry places may have fuzzy leaves. This helps keep water inside the plant.

Some leaves help keep the plant alive. Leaves can be tough or sharp. They can be filled with poison. These leaves keep animals from eating them.

The oak leaf is different from the leaves on a fir tree.

Why do plants need roots and stems?

How Roots Help Plants

Roots hold plants in the ground. They store food for the plant. Roots draw water and minerals out of the soil.

Many plants have a taproot. Taproots are large roots that grow deep in the soil. They store food for the plant. Have you eaten a beet or a carrot? If so, you've tasted a taproot!

Beet

Carrots

Beets and carrots are roots you can eat.

There are small root hairs at the tips of roots. Roots with their many hairs grow deep into the soil. These hairs take in water for the plant.

Tubes carry water to the stem and leaves. The Sun can dry out a plant. On hot days, roots take in water to replace what is lost.

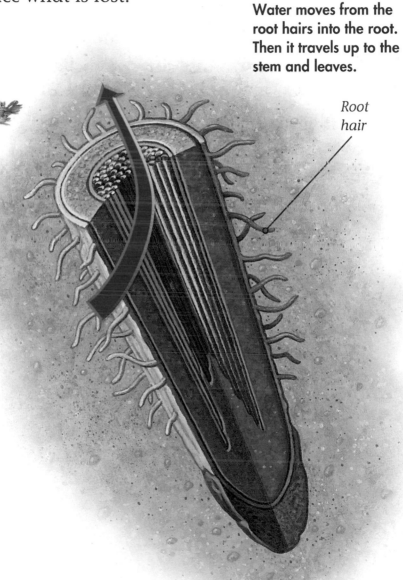

Water moves from the root hairs into the root. Then it travels up to the stem and leaves.

Root hair

How Stems Help Plants

A stem holds up a plant's leaves, fruits, and flowers. Its tubes move water from the roots to the leaves. Other tubes take food from the leaves to the stem and roots.

Some stems are thin and grow along the ground. These stems can grow roots and a new plant.

Cactus stems are fat and have a thick covering. This helps keep water inside the plant.

These cactus plants have spines. The spines are special leaves.

Potatoes are stem parts that grow underground. They store food for the plant. New stems can grow from a potato's buds. The buds are also called "eyes."

Some stems have special parts that keep plants safe. Some stems have hairs that sting animals. Other stems have thorns. Both thorns and stinging hairs help keep animals away.

Potatoes can be eaten. But you must dig them out of the ground.

How are plants grouped?

Flowering Plants

Grasses and trees are types of plants. Trees have a strong, woody stem to hold them up. Grasses do not have woody stems. They grow near the ground.

In the fall, many grasses keep only their roots alive. In the spring they grow a new stem with leaves.

In the fall many trees' leaves die and fall off. These trees are **deciduous.** Deciduous trees grow new leaves in the spring.

These plants and trees both have flowers. The trees are tall. The plants are short.

Making Seeds

Flowers have special parts that make pollen. The petals of a flower attract insects or other animals. They often move the pollen. Wind can also **pollinate** a flower. This happens when pollen is moved to the part of another flower that makes seeds. When a flower is pollinated, seeds form. The seeds are protected by fruit that grows around them.

This bee moves pollen from another plant to the seed-making part of the flower.

Pollen

Seed-making part

Petal

Coniferous Trees

Coniferous trees do not lose their leaves all at once. They do not grow flowers. They have cones that make seeds. The leaves of these trees look like needles. Pine, spruce, hemlock, and fir are coniferous trees.

Two Types of Cones

Coniferous trees make two kinds of cones. One cone is a small pollen cone. The other is a large seed cone. A seed starts to grow when pollen from the pollen cone of another tree attaches to the seed cone. Seeds fall to the ground when they are ripe. Sometimes the seeds grow into trees.

Pollen from these small cones needs to reach seeds in a bigger cone. Wind makes this happen.

Seed

How do new plants grow?

Scattering Seeds

Seeds are scattered so they can grow in new places. Some seeds are scattered by water. Wind can carry seeds that are very light. Animals carry other seeds away. Sometimes animals eat the seed's fruit. The seed passes through the animal's body. Then it is dropped to the ground. Other seeds are scattered when they stick to an animal's fur.

A seed can blow away in the wind.

A seed can stick to fur.

Special Ways of Releasing Seeds

Some types of cones need to be heated by a forest fire. Then the cones can release their seeds. The fire also removes other plants around the trees. This makes space for the seeds to grow.

A seed can float away in water.

A seed can be eaten.

Germinating and Growing

Seeds come in different colors, sizes, and shapes. Every seed has a tiny plant inside it. Every seed also has a seed coat. This protects the plant inside the seed. The tiny plant can grow into a new plant.

Every seed has one or more seed leaves. A **seed leaf** gives food to the new plant.

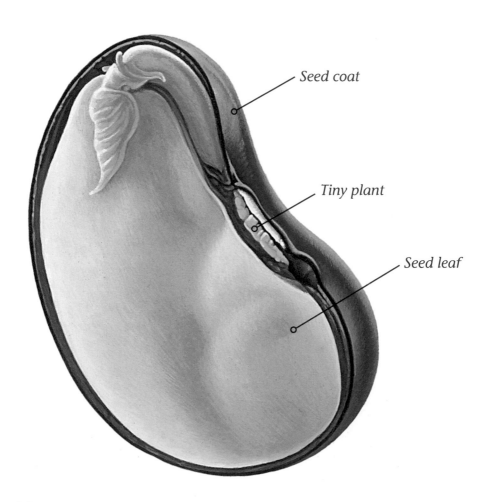

Seed coat

Tiny plant

Seed leaf

Seeds need special things to sprout, or **germinate.** They need air, the right temperature, and enough water. When things are right, a seed sprouts. The seed breaks open and a **seedling,** or young plant, begins to grow. A young root grows down. A stem with leaves grows up. This plant uses food stored in its seed to grow.

This seed has germinated.

This seedling has sprouted. It needs water and sunlight to grow.

Life Cycle of a Plant

First, a seed must germinate. Next, a seedling grows a root downward into the soil. Then, the seedling's stem grows upward. Then the stem grows leaves. Finally, the leaves use sunlight to make sugar for the plant to eat.

Germinating seed

This peanut plant starts out as a seed. What happens next?

Seed

Soon the seedling grows into an adult plant with flowers. The flowers are pollinated and new seeds grow. If the seeds germinate they grow into new plants. Then the cycle starts again.

Seedling

Adult plant

How are plants from the past like today's plants?

Plants That Lived Long Ago

A **fossil** is the remains of a living thing. Fossils come from plants or animals that lived long ago. We can learn about plants by studying fossils.

A fossil forms after a plant dies. The plant gets pressed into mud and rots away. The mud keeps the plant's form. Over time, the mud hardens into rock. When the rock cracks open, you can see the fossil.

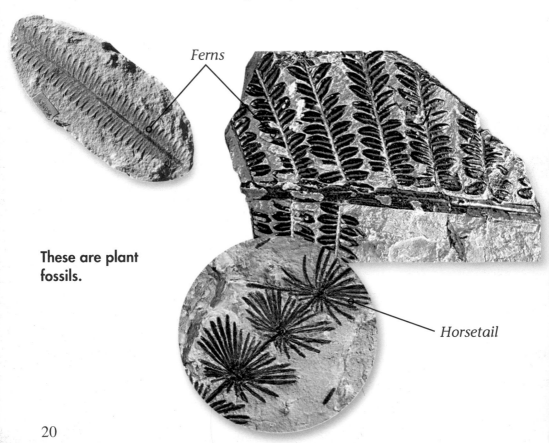

Ferns

Horsetail

These are plant fossils.

Petrified fossils form when rock replaces plant parts. Sometimes a tree gets buried in the ground. Minerals from water replace the tree's wood. Over a long time, the wood becomes stone.

When a plant becomes **extinct,** none of its kind will ever live again. Ferns that live today are different from extinct ferns.

Petrified wood fossils

Plants Change Over Time

By studying fossils, we've learned that the first plants did not have flowers or cones. But plants changed over time. Trees that made cones spread over Earth. Plants with flowers started to grow.

This is a fossil of a magnolia leaf.

Some magnolias bloom all at once in spring. Then new leaves grow.

Magnolias are flowering plants. They have grown and changed over millions of years. Magnolias from long ago kept their leaves year-round. Now, some magnolias lose their leaves in the fall. But magnolia flowers have stayed the same for millions of years.

Plants grow all over the Earth. They grow and live in different ways. Plants make food energy from light energy. Without them, life would be impossible!

Magnolia trees grew on Earth when dinosaurs lived here. Dinosaurs are extinct. Magnolia trees are still found on Earth.

Glossary

coniferous makes seeds in a cone

deciduous loses its leaves in the fall

extinct type of living thing that no longer exists

fossil remains of a living thing from long ago

germinate to begin to grow

pollinate when pollen is moved to a flower part that makes seeds

seed leaf part of a seed that provides food for the new plant

seedling young plant

system a set of parts that work together